Hello, 이솝우화!

개정판

① 1

Hello, 이솝우화! 1 (개정판)

2007년 6월 19일   초판 1쇄 펴냄
2023년 10월 20일 개정판 1쇄 펴냄

원작 이솝
글 국제어학연구소 영어학부편
감수 이동호
그림 유지환·최정현·조한유
펴낸이 이규인
펴낸곳 국제어학연구소 출판부
출판등록 2010년 1월 18일 제302-2010-000006호
주소 서울특별시 마포구 대흥로4길 49, 1층(용강동 월명빌딩)
Tel (02) 704-0900 **팩시밀리** (02) 703-5117
홈페이지 www.bookcamp.co.kr
e-mail changbook1@hanmail.net

ISBN 979-11-9792042-4 (13740)
정가 16,800원

영어의 기초를 다져 주는

magic

Hello,
이솝우화!

1

개정판

원작 이솝 | 글 국제어학연구소 영어학부
감수 이동호 | 그림 유지환·최정현·조한유

ILR 국제어학연구소

이 책의 특징

　　이 책은 아이들에게 친숙한 이솝우화를 영어로 읽으면서, 자연스럽게 영어의 낱말과 표현을 학습하게 하는 책입니다. '이제 막 영어를 배우기 시작한 아이들이 영어문장을 이해할 수 있을까?' 라고 생각할 수도 있을 것입니다. 하지만 이솝우화는 거의 모든 아이들이 이미 알고 있는 이야기입니다. 또한 예쁜 그림으로 설명이 뒷받침되기 때문에, 스토리에 나오는 낱말과 표현을 쉽고도 재미있게 이해할 수 있습니다.

　　이 책은 또한 언어의 습득 과정인 듣기 → 말하기 → 읽기 → 쓰기의 순서대로 학습이 진행됩니다. 이렇게 다양한 방법으로 여러 번 낱말과 표현을 익히게 되면, 쉽게 잊어버리지 않으므로 진정한 자기의 실력이 됩니다.

　　이 책의 목적은 스토리에 나오는 모든 낱말과 표현을 이해하는 것이 아닙니다. 스토리에 나오는 낱말과 표현 중에서도 중요한 낱말과 표현만을 골라 학습하게 합니다.

　　낱말 익히기와 표현 익히기에서 배우게 되는 낱말과 표현만 알아도 상당한 효과를 얻을 수 있습니다. 그러면서도 스토리를 통해서 영어를 익히게 되므로, 기본적인 문장 감각을 몸에 베이게 하는 효과를 볼 수 있습니다.

 부모님! 이렇게 지도해 주세요!

❶ 예비학습

스토리 이후의 학습에서 본격적인 학습이 이루어지므로, 예비학습은 그림을 한 번 보고, 듣는 정도로 가볍게 넘기세요.

❷ 스토리

스토리의 낱말과 문장을 모두 이해하려고 하지 마세요. 낱말과 표현 익히기에서 배우게 되는 낱말과 표현만 확실히 알게 해주셔도 아주 좋은 효과를 얻을 수 있습니다.

❸ 낱말 익히기와 표현 익히기

스토리에서 나온 낱말과 표현을 익히는 과정입니다. 먼저 MP3를 들으면서 따라 말하고, 따라 씁니다. 이 단계에서는 낱말과 표현을 확실하게 익히는 것이 좋으므로, 필요하다면 MP3를 다시 들으면서 다른 노트에 더 써보는 것도 좋은 방법입니다.

이렇게 확실하게 익힌 후에 문제를 풀게 되는데, 듣기 → 말하기 → 읽기 → 쓰기의 순서로 문제를 풀게 되므로, 보다 쉽고 확실하게 낱말과 표현을 확인할 수 있습니다.

❹ 뽀너스! 뽀너스!

사자(lion)와 쥐(mouse)를 영어로 배우면, 호기심 많은 아이들은 '그럼 다른 동물들은 영어로 뭐라고 할까?' 라는 의문이 생기겠죠? 또 '나는 너무 졸려(I'm too sleepy.)' 라는 표현을 배우면, 그럼 '나는 너무 피곤해.' 는 영어로 뭐라고 할까? 라는 의문도 생길 것입니다.

이 단계는 이러한 궁금점을 해소함과 동시에 같은 범주에 있는 새로운 낱말과 표현을 확장해서 배우게 되는 효과가 있습니다.

❺ Dictation

Dictation은 우리말로 '받아쓰기' 라는 말이에요. 이 교재에서는 단순히 영어 낱말이나 표현을 듣고 받아쓰는 것이 아니라, 앞에서 배웠던 스토리를 그림과 함께 보여주면서, 문장의 빈칸을 채워서 쓰도록 합니다. 따라서 스토리에 대한 이해를 함께 할 수 있습니다.

원어민이 천천히 읽기는 하지만, 한 문장 한 문장을 놓치지 않고 집중해야 빈칸에 알맞은 낱말이나 표현을 쓸 수 있습니다. 만일 놓쳤다해도 MP3를 다시 들으면서 끝까지 모두 쓰도록 하세요.

❻ 스토리 이해하기

이제까지의 학습으로 중요 영어 낱말과 표현, 또한 스토리의 내용을 이해하게 되었을 것입니다.

이 단계는 이제까지 학습한 내용을 문장을 통해서 확인해보는 단계입니다.

앞에서 배운 내용보다는 난이도가 있지만, 이제까지 충실하게 교재를 학습했다면 충분히 풀 수 있는 문제들이므로, 자신감을 가지고 도전하세요!

5

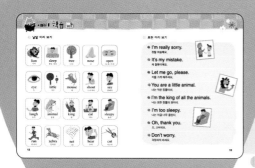

예비학습

스토리를 읽기 전에, 스토리에 나오는
낱말과 표현을 미리 익혀요.

스토리

원어민의 정확한 발음으로 스토리를
들으면서 어떤 내용인지 파악해요.

낱말 익히기와 표현 익히기

원어민의 발음을 그대로 따라 하고, 읽고, 쓰면서
낱말과 표현을 익혀요.

듣기, 말하기, 읽기, 쓰기 문제

앞에서 익힌 낱말과 표현을
듣기 → 말하기 → 읽기 → 쓰기의
순서대로 문제를 풀어요.

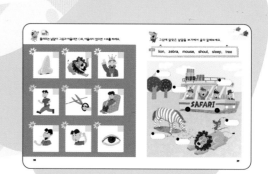

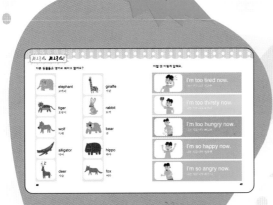

스토리에 나왔던 낱말과 표현 중에서
같은 범주에 속하는 낱말과 표현을 익혀요.

Dictation

스토리를 다시 들으면서,
빈칸에 들어갈 낱말과 표현을 직접 써요.

스토리 이해하기

그림과 문장을 통해서 배운 스토리를
잘 이해하고 있는지 확인해요.

The Lion and the Mouse · 10

The Sun and the Wind · 64

The Country Mouse and the City Mouse · 118

우리말 해석과 정답

The Lion and the MouSe

예비 학습 🔲 MP3

🌸 낱말 미리 보기

lion
사자

sleep
잠을 자다

tree
나무

nose
코

open
(눈을) 뜨다

eye
눈

little
작은

mouse
쥐

shout
소리치다

say
말하다

laugh
웃다

animal
동물

king
왕

eat
먹다

sleepy
졸린

run
달리다

zebra
얼룩말

net
그물

hear
듣다

cut
자르다

※ 표현 미리 보기

- **I'm really sorry.**
  정말 죄송해요.

- **It's my mistake.**
  제 잘못이에요.

- **Let me go, please.**
  저를 가게 해주세요.

- **You are a little animal.**
  너는 작은 동물이야.

- **I'm the king of all the animals.**
  나는 모든 동물의 왕이야.

- **I'm too sleepy.**
  나는 지금 너무 졸린다.

- **Oh, thank you.**
  오, 고마워요.

- **Don't worry.**
  걱정하지 마세요.

The Lion and the Mouse

The **lion** is **sleep**ing under the **tree**.
Suddenly he feels something
touching his **nose**.
He **open**s his **eyes**.
It is a **little mouse**.
The **lion** catches the **mouse**.

"How dare you wake me up!"
shouts the lion.
"I'm really sorry," says the mouse.
"It's my mistake.
Let me go, please."

"I'll pay you back one day,"
says the **mouse**.
The **lion laugh**s, "You'll repay me?
You are a little animal.
And I'm the king of all the animals.
How can you help me?"

"Please, great **king**.

Don't **eat** me," cries the **mouse**.

The **lion** yawns and **say**s,

"OK. I'm too sleepy now.

I'll let you go," **say**s the lion.

"Oh, thank you," **say**s the **mouse**.

"I won't forget your kindness."

And the **mouse run**s away quickly.

A few days later,

the **lion** is following a **zebra**.

Suddenly,

a great **net** comes down on him.

It holds him fast.

The **lion** tries to escape.

But he cannot escape.

The **lion shout**s and **shout**s.

The **mouse** **hears** him.

"That sounds just like the **lion**,"

says the **mouse**.

The **mouse** **run**s to the **lion**.

Soon the **mouse** arrives there.

"Hello, great **king**," **say**s the **mouse**.

"Don't worry.

I'll set you free."

The **mouse** begins to **cut** the **net**.

"There you are," **say**s the **mouse**.

"I told you I'd repay you."

The **lion say**s,

"Thank you, my **little** friend."

낱말을 듣고, 따라 말하고, 따라 써보세요.

lion [láiən] 사자

lion _____ _____

sleep [slíːp] 잠을 자다

sleep _____ _____

tree [triː] 나무

tree _____ _____

nose [nouz] 코

nose _____ _____

open [óupən] (눈을) 뜨다

open _____ _____

eye [ai] 눈

eye _____ _____ _____

little [lítl] 작은

little _____ _____ _____

mouse [maus] 쥐

mouse _____ _____ _____

shout [ʃaut] 소리치다

shout _____ _____ _____

say [sei] 말하다

say _____ _____ _____

laugh [læf] 웃다

laugh

animal [ǽnəməl] 동물

animal

king [kiŋ] 왕

king

eat [iːt] 먹다

eat

sleepy [slíːpi] 졸린

sleepy

run [rʌn] 달리다

run

zebra [zíːbrə] 얼룩말

zebra

net [net] 그물

net

hear [hiər] 듣다

hear

cut [kʌt] 자르다

cut

들려주는 낱말이 그림과 어울리면 ○표, 어울리지 않으면 ×표를 하세요.

그림에 알맞은 낱말을 보기에서 골라 말해보세요.

lion, zebra, mouse, shout, sleep, tree

그림을 보고, 알맞은 낱말을 골라 동그라미하세요.

1

lion | mouse

2

hear | say

3
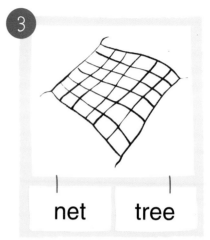
net | tree

4

king | zebra

5

eat | sleepy

6

laugh | cut

7

nose | animal

8

run | open

9
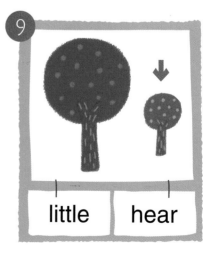
little | hear

우리말을 보고, 영어 낱말의 빈칸에 알맞은 알파벳을 쓰세요.

① 나무   t □ ee   ② 눈   e □ e

③ 왕   ki □ g   ④ 먹다   □ at

⑤ 그물   ne □   ⑥ 얼룩말   □ ebra

⑦ 웃다   l □ ugh   ⑧ 듣다   he □ r

⑨ 말하다   sa □   ⑩ 사자   lio □

⑪ 잠을 자다   s □ ee □   ⑫ 쥐   □ ous □

⑬ 코   no □ e   ⑭ 소리치다   sho □ t

⑮ (눈을)뜨다   □ pen   ⑯ 동물   an □ ma □

⑰ 작은   littl □   ⑱ 졸린   □ lee □ y

⑲ 자르다   □ ut   ⑳ 달리다   r □ n

표현을 듣고, 따라 말하고, 따라 쓰세요.

● **I'm really sorry.** 정말 죄송해요.

I'm really sorry.

● **It's my mistake.** 제 잘못이에요.

It's my mistake.

● **Let me go, please.** 저를 가게 해주세요.

Let me go, please.

● **You are a little animal.** 너는 작은 동물이야.

You are a little animal.

● **I'm the king of all the animals.** 나는 모든 동물의 왕이야.

I'm the king of all the animals.

● **I'm too sleepy.** 나는 지금 너무 졸린다.

<u>I'm too sleepy.</u>

_____

● **Oh, thank you.** 오, 고마워요.

<u>Oh, thank you.</u>

_____

● **Don't worry.** 걱정하지 마세요.

<u>Don't worry.</u>

_____

✳ **명령문**

상대방에게 '~을 하라'라고 지시할 때의 문장은 동사의 원형으로 시작해요.
또 '~을 하지 마라'라고 지시할 때의 문장은 Don't 으로 시작해요.

· Open your eyes.   눈을 뜨세요.
· Don't open your eyes.   눈을 뜨지 마세요.
· Don't worry.   걱정하지 마세요.
· Don't eat me.   저를 먹지 마세요.

43

그림을 보고, 들려주는 표현 중에서 알맞은 것을 고르세요.

1. a □ b □

2. a □ b □

3. a □ b □

4. a □ b □

5. a □ b □

그림에 알맞은 표현을 보기에서 골라 말해보세요.

I'm the king of all the animals.   I'm too sleepy.

Let me go, please.   Oh, thank you.

그림과 문장이 서로 어울리도록 연결하세요.

① 　　　　　•　　　🌸 Let me go, please.

② 　　　　　•　　　🌸 I'm too sleepy.

③ 　　　　　•　　　🌸 I'm really sorry.

④ 　　　　　•　　　🌸 Oh, thank you.

⑤ 　　　　　•　　　🌸 You are a little animal.

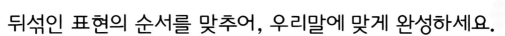

뒤섞인 표현의 순서를 맞추어, 우리말에 맞게 완성하세요.

① 제 실수예요. my it's mistake

→ _____

② 저를 가게 해 주세요. me go let please

→ _____

③ 걱정하지 마세요. worry don't

→ _____

④ 나는 모든 동물의 왕이다. of all the king the animals I'm

→ _____

⑤ 정말 죄송해요. really I'm sorry

→ _____

다른 동물들은 영어로 뭐라고 할까요?

elephant
코끼리

giraffe
기린

tiger
호랑이

rabbit
토끼

wolf
늑대

bear
곰

alligator
악어

hippo
하마

deer
사슴

fox
여우

이럴 땐 이렇게 말해요.

I'm too tired now.
나는 지금 너무 피곤해.

I'm too thirsty now.
나는 지금 너무 목말라.

I'm too hungry now.
나는 지금 너무 배고파.

I'm so happy now.
나는 지금 너무 행복해.

I'm so angry now.
나는 지금 너무 화가 나.

Dictation

스토리를 들으면서 빈칸에 빠진 부분을 쓰세요.

The lion is sleeping under the ❶_____.

Suddenly he feels something touching his ❷_____.

He opens his ❸_____s.

It is a little ❹_____.

The lion catches the mouse.

50

"How dare you wake me up!"

⑤ _____s the lion.

" ⑥ _____ ," says the mouse.

"It's my mistake.

⑦ _____ "

"I'll pay you back one day," says the mouse .

The lion ①_____s, "You'll repay me?

You are a ②_____ animal.

And I'm the ③_____ of all the animals.

How can you help me?"

"Please, great king.

Don't ④ _____ me," cries the mouse.

The lion yawns and says.

"OK. ⑤ _____

I'll let you go," says the lion.

MP3

"①_____," says the mouse.

"I won't forget your kindness."

And the mouse ②_____s away quickly.

A few days later,

the lion is following a ③ _____.

Suddenly,

a great ④ _____ comes down on him.

It holds him fast.

The lion tries to escape.

But he cannot escape.

The lion ❶ _____s and ❷ _____s.

The mouse ③_____s him.

"That sounds just like the lion,"

says the mouse.

The mouse ④_____s to the lion.

Soon the mouse arrives there.

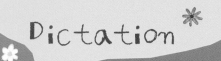

"Hello, great king," says the mouse.

" ① _____

I'll set you free."

The mouse begins to ② _____ the net.

58

"There you are," says the ③ _____.

"I told you I'd repay you."

The ④ _____ says,

"Thank you, my ⑤ _____ friend."

A 그림을 보고, 알맞은 문장에 ○표를 하고, 틀린 문장에는 ×표 하세요.

1

① The mouse is sleeping under the tree. (   )

② The lion opens his eyes. (   )

③ It is a little king. (   )

2

① The mouse hears him. (   )

② The mouse runs to the zebra. (   )

③ And the mouse yawns and says. (   )

B 그림의 내용을 가장 잘 표현한 문장을 고르세요.

1

① The lion tries to eat.

② The lion tries to escape.

③ The mouse tries to escape.

① The lion begins to yawn.

② The lion begins to cut the net.

③ The mouse begins to cut the net.

C 그림의 내용을 보고, 빈칸에 알맞은 낱말을 보기에서 골라 쓰세요.

eat, zebra, king, net, sleepy, say

1.

"Please, great ❶ _____."
"Don't ❷ _____ me.
The lion yawns and ❸ _____s.
OK. I'm too ❹ _____ now.

2.

The lion is following a ❶ _____.
Suddenly, a great ❷ _____ comes down on him.

D 주어진 표현을 이용하여 그림의 내용에 맞도록 문장을 쓰세요.

①

얼룩말이 잠을 자고 있다.
(the / sleeping / zebra / is)

➡ _____

②

쥐가 하품을 한다.
(mouse / yawns / the)

➡ _____

③

고양이가 쥐를 쫓아가고 있어요.
(is following / the mouse / the cat)

➡ _____

④

개가 탈출하려고 해요.
(the dog / escape / tries to)

➡ _____

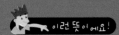 이런 뜻이에요!

 예비 학습   듣기   말하기   읽기   쓰기

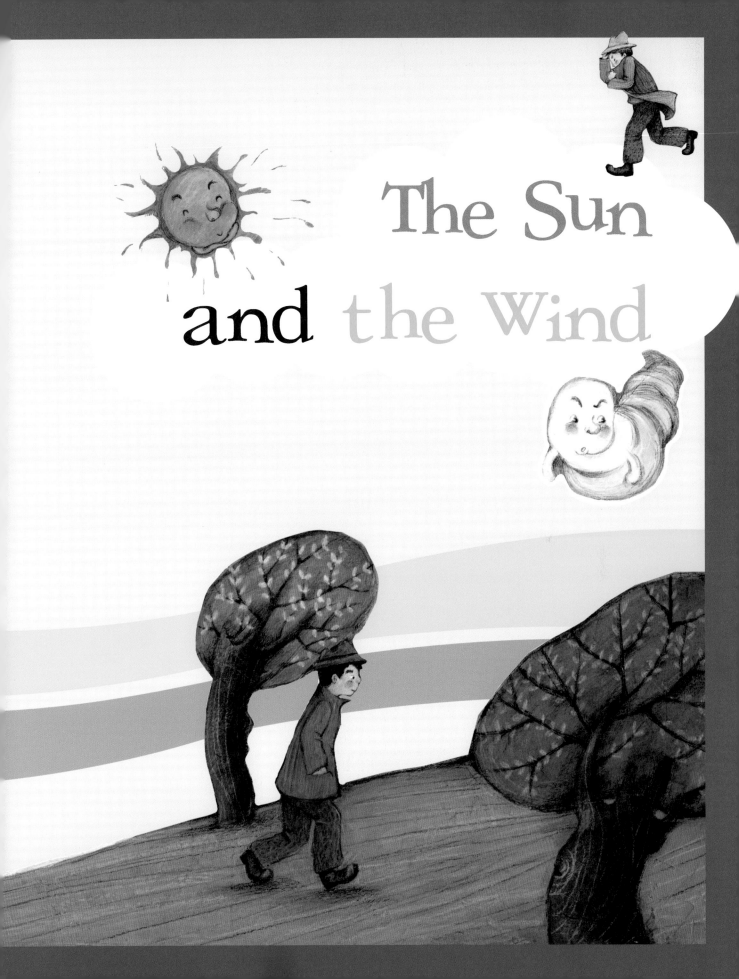

The Sun and the Wind

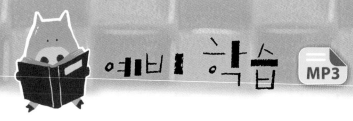
✿ 낱말 미리 보기

sun
해

wind
바람

house
집

ship
배

sea
바다

flower
꽃

grow
자라다

child
어린이

test
시험

man
남자

walk
걷다

road
길

coat
외투

face
얼굴

red
빨간색

tomato
토마토

hat
모자

socks
양말

shoes
구두

water
물

※ 표현 미리 보기

● **I'm stronger than you.**
나는 너보다 강해.

● **I can break down a house.**
나는 집을 무너뜨릴 수 있어.

● **What can you do?**
너는 무엇을 할 수 있니?

● **I help the trees to grow.**
나는 나무를 자라게 도와.

● **I'd beat you.**
나는 너를 이길 거야.

● **Let's have a match.**
우리 시합을 하자.

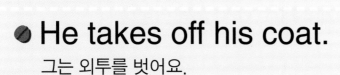

● **My turn.**
내 차례야.

● **He takes off his coat.**
그는 외투를 벗어요.

The Sun and the Wind

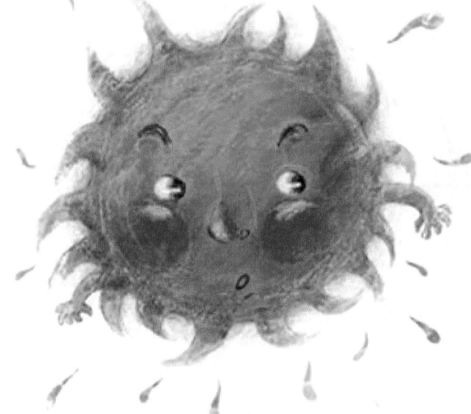

The **sun** and the **wind**
are arguing with each other.
"I'm stronger than you," says the **sun**.
"I'm much stronger than you,"
says the **wind**.

"I can break down a house,"

says the **wind**.

"And I can blow a **ship** across the **sea**.

What can you do?" asks the **wind**.

"That isn't my style," says the **sun**.

"I can make the **flower**s bloom.

And I help the trees to grow."

"Pah! That's **child**'s play,"

says the **wind**.

"In a **test** of strength, I'd beat you."

The **wind** sees a **man**
walking along the **road**.
The **wind** says, "Let's have a match.
Whoever takes off that **man's coat** wins."
"All right," says the **sun**.

"I'll start first," says the **wind**.

"He will take off his **coat** soon."

And the **wind** blows a powerful **wind**.

But the **man** grabs his **coat** tightly.

The **wind** takes a deep breath.

And the **wind** blows with all his energy.

But the **man** grabs his **coat** tighter.

At last, the **wind** gives up.

"My turn," says the **sun**.

And the **sun** begins to shine.

The **man** feels hotter and hotter.

His **face** is as **red** as a **tomato**.

He can't stand any more heat.

So he takes off his coat.

He also takes off his **hat**.

He arrives at a lake.

He takes off his **socks** and **shoes**.

And he dives into the **water**.

"Well?" says the **sun** with a smiling **face**.

"All right, all right," says the **wind**.

"You win."

The **wind** disappears.

낱말 익히기 　낱말을 듣고, 따라 말하고, 따라 써보세요.

sun [sʌn] 해
sun _____ _____

wind [wind] 바람
wind _____ _____

house [haus] 집
house _____ _____

ship [ʃip] 배
ship _____ _____

sea [siː] 바다
sea _____ _____

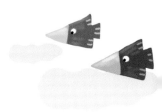

flower [fláuər] 꽃

flower _____ _____ _____

grow [grou] 자라다

grow _____ _____ _____

child [tʃaild] 어린이

child _____ _____ _____

test [test] 시험

test _____ _____ _____

man [mæn] 남자

man _____ _____ _____

walk [wɔːk] 걷다

walk _____ _____

road [roud] 길

road _____ _____

coat [kout] 외투

coat _____ _____

face [feis] 얼굴

face _____ _____

red [red] 빨간색

red _____ _____

tomato [təméitou] 토마토
tomato _____ _____ _____

hat [hæt] 모자
hat _____ _____ _____

socks [sɑks] 양말
socks _____ _____ _____

shoes [ʃuːz] 구두
shoes _____ _____ _____

water [wɔ́ːtər] 물
water _____ _____ _____

들려주는 낱말에 맞는 그림을 골라 동그라미하세요.

그림에 알맞은 낱말을 보기에서 골라 말해보세요.

sea, sun, child, house, man, road, ship

1

2

3

4

5

6

7

그림에 해당하는 낱말만을 골라 동그라미하고, 그 낱말을 쓰세요.

1

g(child)s

child

2

ocoatu

3

estomato

4

shate

5

testes

6

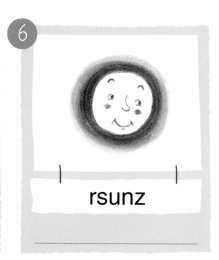

rsunz

7

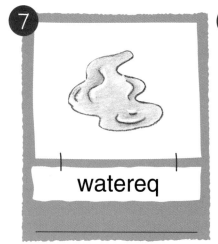

watereq

8

fngrow

9

flowerxs

가로와 세로 열쇠를 보고, 낱말 퍼즐을 풀어보세요.

가로열쇠 ③해 ④빨간색 ⑦신발 ⑧물 ⑪토마토 ⑬걷다 ⑭어린이 ⑯바다 ⑱얼굴 ⑲배 ⑳자라다

세로열쇠 ①집 ②시험 ⑤모자 ⑥길 ⑨남자 ⑩바람 ⑫외투 ⑮양말 ⑰꽃

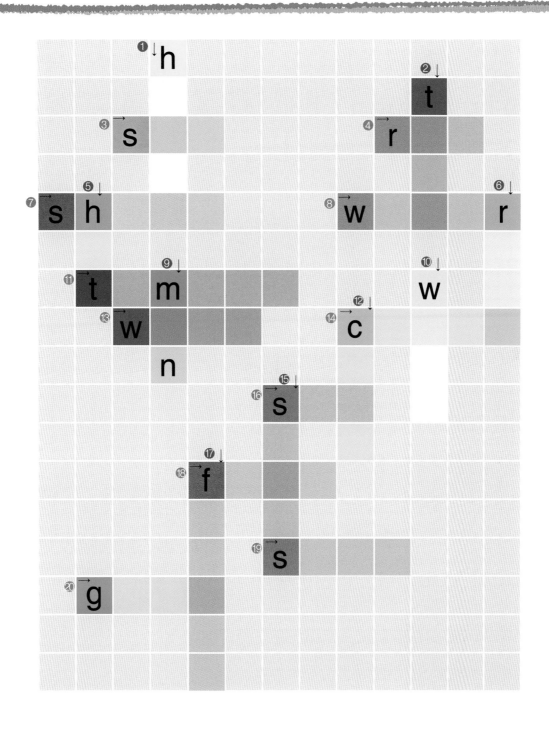

표현 익히기　　표현을 듣고, 따라 말하고, 따라 쓰세요.

● **I'm stronger than you.** 나는 너보다 강해.

<u>I'm stronger than you.</u>

_____

● **I can break down a house.** 나는 집을 무너뜨릴 수 있어.

<u>I can break down a house.</u>

_____

● **What can you do?** 너는 무엇을 할 수 있니?

<u>What can you do?</u>

_____

● **I help the trees to grow.** 나는 나무를 자라게 도와.

<u>I help the trees to grow.</u>

_____

● **I'd beat you.** 나는 너를 이길 거야.

<u>I'd beat you.</u>

_____

Let's have a match. 우리 시합을 하자.

<u>Let's have a match.</u>

_____

My turn. 내 차례야.

<u>My turn.</u>

_____

He takes off his coat. 그는 외투를 벗어요.

<u>He takes off his coat.</u>

_____

'가능' 의 표현

'~할 수 있다'를 표현할 때는 동사 앞에 can을 써서 표현해요. can 뒤에 이어지는 동사는 항상 원형을 쓰고요.

- I can **break down a house.**   나는 집을 무너뜨릴 수 있어.
- I can **help you.**   나는 너를 도울 수 있어.
- I can **run fast.**   나는 빨리 달릴 수 있어.
- I can **make net.**   나는 그물을 만들 수 있어.

들려주는 표현이 어울리는 그림을 골라 순서대로 번호를 쓰세요.

그림에 알맞은 표현을 보기에서 골라 말해보세요.

Let's have a match.   My turn.
I'm stronger than you.   I help the trees to grow.

그림과 문장이 서로 어울리도록 알맞은 낱말을 골라 동그라미하세요.

He takes off his hat .
(coat)

Let's have a match .
eat

I'm stronger than you.
start

I help the flower to grow.
trees

뒤섞인 표현의 순서를 맞추어, 우리말에 맞게 완성하세요.

① 너는 무엇을 할 수 있니? **can** **do** **what** **you**

→ _____

② 나는 집을 무너뜨릴 수 있어. **a house** **down** **can break** **I**

→ _____

③ 나는 너보다 강해. **stronger** **I'm** **than** **you**

→ _____

④ 나는 너를 이길 거야. **beat** **you** **I'd**

→ _____

⑤ 그는 그의 외투를 벗어요. **his coat** **he** **takes off**

→ _____

다른 옷의 이름은 뭐라고 할까요?

shirt
셔츠

skirt
치마

dress
드레스

pants
바지

blouse
블라우스

gloves
장갑

boots
부츠

muffler
머플러

jeans
청바지

sneakers
운동화

이럴 땐 이렇게 말해요.

 I'm taller than you.
나는 너보다 더 키가 커.

 I'm shorter than you.
나는 너보다 더 키가 작아.

 I'm older than you.
나는 너보다 나이가 많아.

 I'm younger than you.
나는 너보다 어려.

 I'm bigger than you.
나는 너보다 덩치가 커.

 I'm smaller than you.
나는 너보다 덩치가 작아.

스토리를 들으면서 빈칸에 빠진 부분을 쓰세요.

The ❶_____ and the wind

are arguing with each other.

"❷_____," says the sun.

"I'm much stronger than you,"

says the ❸_____.

"I can break down a ④_____,"

says the wind.

And I can blow a ship across the ⑤_____."

"⑥_____" asks the wind.

"That isn't my style," says the sun.

"I can make the ①_____s bloom.

And I help the trees to ②_____."

"Pah! That's child's play," says the wind.

"In a test of strength, ③_____."

The wind sees a ④_____

walking along the ⑤_____.

The wind says, "⑥_____

Whoever takes off that man's coat wins."

"All right," says the ⑦_____.

"I'll start first," says the wind.

"He will take off his ❶ _____ soon."

And the wind blows a powerful ❷ _____.

But the man grabs his coat tightly.

The wind takes a deep breath.

And the wind blows with all his energy.

But the ③ _____ grabs his coat tighter.

At last, the ④ _____ gives up.

Dictation

" ①_____," says the sun.

And the ②_____ begins to shine.

The ③_____ feels hotter and hotter.

His ④ _____ is as red as a ⑤ _____ .

He can't stand any more heat.

So ⑥ _____ .

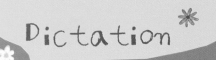

He also takes off his ❶_____.

He arrives at a lake.

He takes off his ❷_____ and ❸_____.

And he dives into the ❹_____.

112

"Well?" says the sun with a smiling ⑤ _____.

"All right, all right," says the wind.

"You win."

The ⑥ _____ disappears.

113

A 그림을 보고, 알맞은 문장에 ○표를 하고, 틀린 문장에는 ✕표 하세요.

①

① "I'll start first", says the sun. (   )

② And the wind begins to blow a powerful wind. (   )

③ But the man grabs his shoes tightly. (   )

②

① He also takes off his hat. (   )

② He arrives at a mountain. (   )

③ He takes off his socks and shoes. (   )

B 그림의 내용을 가장 잘 표현한 문장을 고르세요.

1

① The wind sees a house on the road.

② The wind sees a man walking along the road.

③ The wind sees a child walking along the road.

 2

① He takes off his hat.

② He takes off his coat.

③ He is running along the road.

C 그림의 내용을 보고, 빈칸에 알맞은 낱말을 보기에서 골라 쓰세요.

ship, wind, child, flower, can, grow

1

"I ❶ _____ break down a house," says the wind.

And I can blow a ❷ _____ across the sea."

"What can you do?" asks the ❸ _____.

2

"I can make the ❶ _____s bloom.

And I help the trees to ❷ _____."

"Pah! That's ❸ _____'s play," says the wind.

D 주어진 표현을 이용하여 그림의 내용에 맞도록 문장을 쓰세요.

아이가 양말을 벗는다.
(takes off / his socks / the child)

➜ _____

한 남자가 바다에 도착한다.
(the sea / arrives at / a man)

➜ _____

그녀는 그녀의 모자를 곧 벗을 거야.
(her hat / she / will / take off)

➜ _____

나는 너보다 키가 커.
(you / than / I'm / taller)

➜ _____

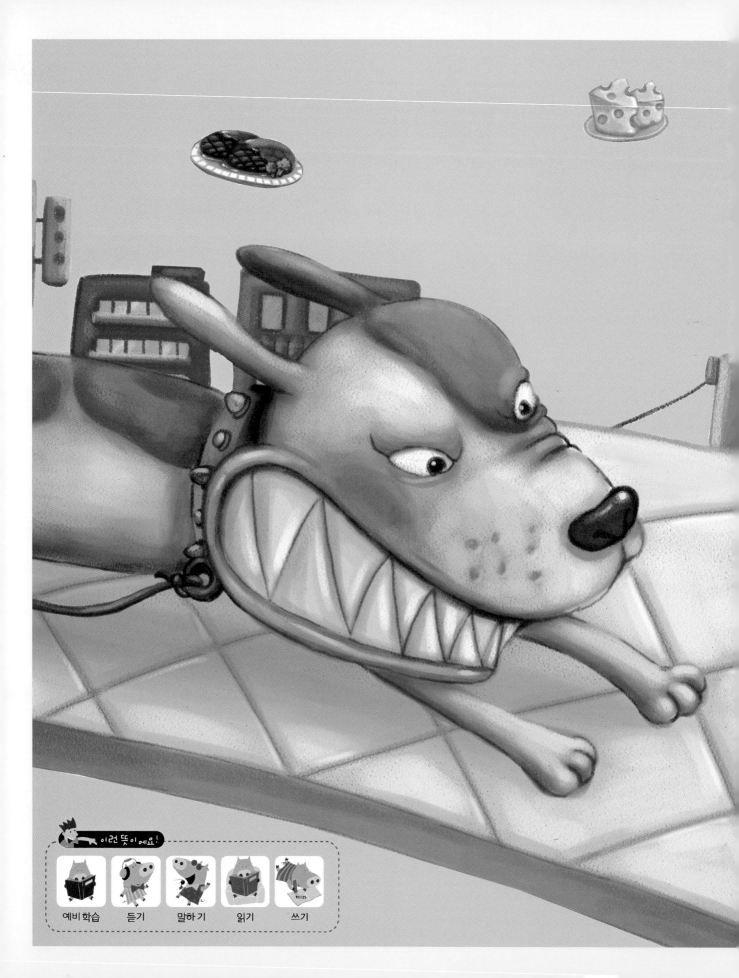

이런 뜻이에요!

예비 학습　　듣기　　말하기　　읽기　　쓰기

The Country Mouse and the City Mouse

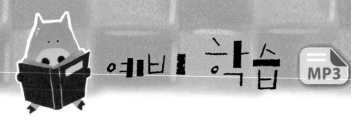

예비 학습 MP3

❀ 낱말 미리 보기

country
시골

city
도시

cousin
사촌

write
쓰다

letter
편지

bean
콩

fruit
과일

hungry
배고픈

food
음식

woods
숲

car
자동차

dog
개

big
커다란

kitchen
부엌

cake
케이크

meat
고기

cheese
치즈

door
문

table
탁자

small
작은

◉ Welcome to my home.

우리 집에 온 걸 환영해.

◉ Help yourself.

많이 먹어.

◉ I don't like this plain food.

나는 이런 평범한 음식은 싫어.

◉ Let's go to the city.

우리 도시로 가자.

◉ It's too dangerous here.

여기는 너무 위험해.

◉ What a big house!

정말 큰 집이다!

◉ It looks delicious.

맛있어 보여.

◉ I'll go back to the country.

나는 시골로 돌아갈 거야.

The Country Mouse
and the City Mouse

The **country** mouse
and the **city** mouse are **cousins**.
One day, the **country** mouse
invites his **cousin**.
He **writes** a **letter**. "Come to my house."

The **city** mouse wears nice clothes.

And he visits the **country** mouse.

The **country** mouse greets him.

"Welcome to my home."

124

The **country** mouse puts out
some **bean**s and **fruit**.
"You must be **hungry**. Help yourself."
The **city** mouse eats the **food**.
But he thinks,
"I don't like this plain food."

After lunch,
they take a walk in the **wood**s.
The **city** mouse thinks,
"It's too dull in the **country**."
He says, "Let's go to the city."

The **country** mouse goes to the **city**.

He sees lots of **car**s.

The **country** mouse thinks,

"It's too dangerous here."

They walk through the streets.

Suddenly, a **dog** runs after them.

They run away from the **dog**.

At last, they arrive at his house.

He lives in a **big** house.

"What a big house!"

says the **country** mouse.

134

They go to the **kitchen**.

There is a **cake**, **meat**, and **cheese**.

The **city** mouse says, "Help yourself."

"Thank you. It looks delicious."

The **country** mouse begins to eat.

Just then, someone opens the **door**.

And people come to the **table**.

The **city** mouse shouts, "Follow me!"

They run away to a **small** hole.

The **country** mouse says,

"I'll go back to the country.

Though I eat only **bean**s,

I want to have a peaceful life."

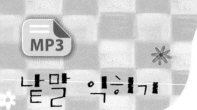

낱말 익히기 낱말을 듣고, 따라 말하고, 따라 써보세요.

country [kʌ́ntri] 시골

country _____ _____

city [síti] 도시

city _____ _____

cousin [kʌ́zn] 사촌

cousin _____ _____

write [rait] 쓰다

write _____ _____

letter [létər] 편지

letter _____ _____

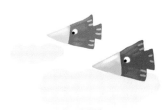

bean [biːn] 콩

bean

fruit [fruːt] 과일

fruit

hungry [hʌ́ŋgri] 배고픈

hungry

food [fuːd] 음식

food

woods [wudz] 숲

woods

car [kɑːr] 자동차

car _____ _____

dog [dɔg] 개

dog _____ _____

big [big] 큰

big _____ _____

kitchen [kítʃən] 부엌

kitchen _____ _____

cake [keik] 케이크

cake _____ _____

meat [miːt] 고기

meat _____ _____

cheese [tʃiːz] 치즈

cheese _____ _____

door [dɔːr] 문

door _____ _____

table [téibəl] 탁자

table _____ _____

small [smɔːl] 작은

small _____ _____

그림을 보고, 들려주는 낱말 중에서 알맞은 것을 고르세요.

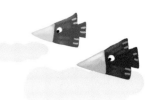

그림에 알맞은 낱말을 보기에서 골라 말해보세요.

fruit, hungry, dog, big, small, cake, cheese

1

2

3

4

5

6

7

그림을 보고 알맞은 낱말을 골라 동그라미하세요.

1

cousin　couson

2

dig　dog

3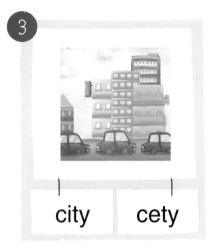

city　cety

4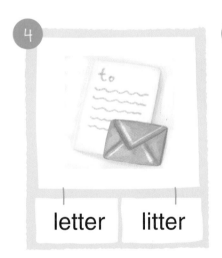

letter　litter

5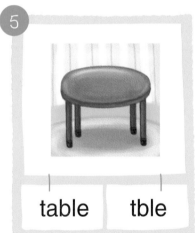

table　tble

6

hungry　hurry

7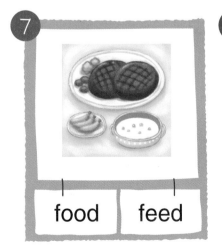

food　feed

8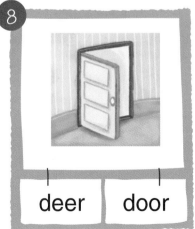

deer　door

9

smell　small

148

연결된 낱말 띠에서 우리말에 해당하는 낱말을 찾아 동그라미하고, 우리말 옆에 다시 쓰세요.

gcountrysegegcousinlepletterzsoobeanlqo

1 시골   country

2 사촌 _____

3 편지 _____

4 콩 _____

fruitsqsebwhungrysqagfoodwgessrcarors

5 과일 _____

6 배고픈 _____

7 음식 _____

8 자동차 _____

doorwmoatablerwuertyesmallwourdogbor

9 문 _____

10 탁자 _____

11 작은 _____

12 개 _____

sbcitybqvahpkitchenscheeseuptymvwritex

13 도시 _____

14 부엌 _____

15 치즈 _____

16 쓰다 _____

esbigohzmwcakehboncpmeatobncnwoodse

17 커다란 _____

18 케이크 _____

19 고기 _____

20 숲 _____

149

표현 익히기 표현을 듣고, 따라 말하고, 따라 쓰세요.

- **Welcome to my home.**
  우리 집에 온 걸 환영해.

  Welcome to my home.
  _____

- **Help yourself.** 많이 먹어.

  Help yourself.
  _____

- **I don't like this plain food.** 나는 이런 평범한 음식은 싫어.

  I don't like this plain food.
  _____

- **Let's go to the city.** 우리 도시로 가자.

  Let's go to the city.
  _____

- **It's too dangerous here.** 여기는 너무 위험해.

  It's too dangerous here.
  _____

What a big house! 정말 큰 집이다!

What a big house!

It looks delicious. 맛있어 보여.

It looks delicious.

I'll go back to the country. 나는 시골로 돌아갈 거야.

I'll go back to the country.

✻ **미래 표현**

'~할 거야'를 표현할 때는 동사 앞에 will을 써서 표현해요. 줄여서 I'll로 많이 써요.
will 다음에는 항상 동사의 원형이 함께 쓰인답니다!

- I'll go back to the country. 나는 시골로 돌아갈 거야.
- I'll go to school. 나는 학교에 갈 거야.
- I'll write a letter. 나는 편지를 쓸 거야.
- I'll eat fruit. 나는 과일을 먹을 거야.

들려주는 표현 중에서 어울리는 그림을 골라 (a) 또는 (b)를 쓰세요.

152

 그림에 알맞은 표현을 보기에서 골라 말해보세요.

보기

Welcome to my home.   Help yourself.
What a big house!   It looks delicious.

1

2

그림에 어울리는 표현을 골라 동그라미하세요.

1
① It looks delicious. ☐

② I don't like this plain food. ☐

2
① Welcome to my home. ☐

② Let's go to the city. ☐

3
① Help yourself. ☐

② I'll go back to the country. ☐

4
① What a big house! ☐

② It's too dangerous here. ☐

뒤섞인 표현의 순서를 맞추어, 우리말에 맞게 완성하세요.

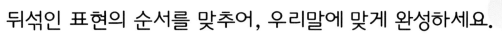

① 우리 도시로 가자. go　Let's　to the city

➜ _____

② 정말 커다란 집이다! big　house　What　a

➜ _____

③ 맛있어 보인다. delicious　looks　it

➜ _____

④ 여기는 너무 위험해. dangerous　too　it's　here

➜ _____

⑤ 우리 집에 온 것을 환영해. to　my home　welcome

➜ _____

다른 음식의 이름은 뭐라고 할까요?

sandwich
샌드위치

bread
빵

hot dog
핫도그

doughnut
도너츠

hot cake
핫케이크

pizza
피자

spaghetti
스파게티

coffee
커피

milk
우유

juice
주스

이럴 땐 이렇게 말해요.

What a big animal!
정말 큰 동물이다.

What a small animal!
정말 작은 동물이다!

What a tall boy!
정말 큰 소년이다!

What a short boy!
정말 작은 소년이다!

What a new house!
정말 새 집이다!

What an old house!
정말 오래된 집이다!

Dictation

스토리를 들으면서 빈칸에 빠진 부분을 쓰세요.

The ① _____ mouse

and the city mouse are cousins.

One day, the country ② _____

invites his cousin.

He writes a letter, "Come to my house."

The ③ _____ mouse wears nice clothes.

And he visits the ④ _____ mouse.

The country mouse greets him.

"⑤ _____"

The country mouse puts out
some beans and ❶ _____ .
"You must be hungry. ❷ _____ "
The city mouse eats the ❸ _____ .
But he thinks, "I don't like this plain food."

After lunch,

they take a walk in the ④ _____ .

The city ⑤ _____ thinks,

"It's too dull in the country."

He says, " ⑥ _____ "

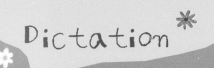

The country mouse goes to the ① _____ .

He sees lots of ② _____ s.

The ③ _____ mouse thinks,

" ④ _____ "

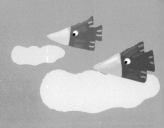

They ⑤ _____ through the streets.

Suddenly, a ⑥ _____ runs after them.

They run away from the dog.

At last, they arrive at his house.

He lives in a ① _____ house.

" ② _____ "

says the country ③ _____ .

They go to the ④_____.

There is a ⑤_____, meat, and ⑥_____.

The city mouse says, "Help yourself."

"Thank you. ⑦_____"

The country mouse begins to eat.

Just then, someone opens the ❶ _____ .

And people come to the ❷ _____ .

The city mouse shouts, "Follow me!"

They run away to a ❸ _____ hole.

The country mouse says,

"I'll go back to the ④_____.

Though I eat only ⑤_____s,

I want to have a peaceful life."

A 그림을 보고, 알맞은 문장에 ○표를 하고, 틀린 문장에는 ✕표 하세요.

①

① The city mouse wears nice clothes. (　　)

② He visits the country mouse. (　　)

③ The city mouse greets him. (　　)

②

① The country mouse puts out some cake. (　　)

② The city mouse eats the food. (　　)

③ But he thinks, "It looks delicious." (　　)

B 그림의 내용을 가장 잘 표현한 문장을 고르세요.

① They goes to the city.

② They run away from the dog.

③ They take a walk in the woods.

① A dog runs after them.

② People come to the table.

③ A dog runs away to a small hole.

C 그림의 내용을 보고, 빈칸에 알맞은 내용을 보기에서 골라 쓰세요.

보기 car, run, walk, country, dog, city

1

The country mouse goes to the ❶_____.

He sees lots of ❷_____s .

The ❸_____ mouse thinks, "It's too dangerous here."

2

They ❶_____ through the streets.

Suddenly, a ❷_____ runs after them.

They ❸_____ away from the dog.

D 주어진 표현을 이용하여 그림의 내용에 맞도록 문장을 쓰세요.

1.

   아이가 문을 연다.
   (opens / the door / the child)

   ➜ _____

2.

   그는 편지를 쓴다.
   (writes / he / a letter)

   ➜ _____

3.

   그들은 숲 속을 산책한다.
   (take a walk / they / in the woods)

   ➜ _____

4.

   그들은 개한테 쫓겨 도망을 간다.
   (run away / from the dog / they)

   ➜ _____

The Lion and the Mouse

⟨14p-15p⟩

The lion is sleeping under the tree.
Suddenly he feels something touching his nose.
He opens his eyes.
It is a little mouse.
The lion catches the mouse.

사자가 나무 아래에서 잠을 자고 있어요.
갑자기 사자는 그의 코에 뭔가가 닿는 것을 느껴요.

사자는 눈을 떠요.
그것은 작은 쥐예요.
사자는 쥐를 잡아요.

⟨16p-17p⟩

"How dare you wake me up!" shouts the lion.
"I'm really sorry," says the mouse.
"It's my mistake.
Let me go, please."

"감히 나를 깨우다니." 사자가 소리쳐요.
"정말 죄송합니다." 쥐가 말해요.
"제 실수예요.
 제발, 저를 보내주세요."

⟨18p-19p⟩

"I'll pay you back one day," says the mouse.
The lion laughs, "You'll repay me?
You are a little animal.
And I'm the king of all the animals.
How can you help me?"

"언젠가 당신에게 은혜를 갚겠어요." 쥐가 말해요.
사자는 웃어요. "나에게 은혜를 갚겠다고?
너는 작은 동물이야.
그리고 나는 모든 동물들의 왕이고.
어떻게 나를 돕겠느냐?"

⟨20p-21p⟩

"Please, great king.
Don't eat me," cries the mouse.
The lion yawns and says,
"OK. I'm too sleepy now.
 I'll let you go," says the lion.

"제발, 위대한 왕이시여.
저를 먹지 마세요." 쥐가 울어요.
사자는 하품을 하고 말을 해요.
"좋다. 나는 지금 너무 졸린다.
 너를 보내주마." 사자가 말해요.

⟨22p-23p⟩

"Oh, thank you," says the mouse.
"I won't forget your kindness."
And the mouse runs away quickly.

"오, 감사합니다." 쥐가 말해요.
"당신의 친절을 잊지 않겠어요."
그리고 쥐는 빨리 도망을 가요.

〈24p-25p〉

A few days later,
the lion is following a zebra.
Suddenly, a great net comes down on him.
It holds him fast.

며칠 후에,
사자는 얼룩말을 따라가고 있어요.
갑자기, 커다란 그물이 사자에게 떨어져요.
그물은 사자를 빠르게 묶어요.

〈26p-27p〉

The lion tries to escape.
But he cannot escape.
The lion shouts and shouts.

사자는 도망치려고 해요.
하지만 도망칠 수가 없어요.
사자는 소리치고 또 소리쳐요.

〈28p-29p〉

The mouse hears him.
"That sounds just like the lion,"
says the mouse.
The mouse runs to the lion.
Soon the mouse arrives there.

쥐는 그 소리를 들어요.
"저 소리는 사자님의 소리 같아."
쥐는 말해요.
쥐는 사자에게로 달려가요.
곧 쥐는 그 곳에 도착해요.

〈30p-31p〉

"Hello, great king," says the mouse.
"Don't worry.
 I'll set you free."
The mouse begins to cut the net.

"안녕하세요, 위대한 왕이시여." 쥐가 말해요.
"걱정하지 마세요.
 제가 당신을 자유롭게 해 드릴게요."
쥐는 그물을 끊기 시작해요.

〈32p-33p〉

"There you are," says the mouse.
"I told you I'd repay you."
The lion says,
"Thank you, my little friend."

"됐어요." 쥐가 말해요.
"제가 은혜를 갚겠다고 말했죠."
사자는 말해요.
"고맙다, 내 작은 친구야."

173

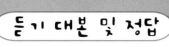

듣기 대본 및 정답

낱말 익히기

🐸 듣기 문제 ················· 38p

(듣기대본)

❶ nose ❷ mouse ❸ king
❹ eat ❺ cut ❻ sleepy
❼ zebra ❽ hear ❾ tree

정답

❶ ○   ❷ ✕   ❸ ○
❹ ✕   ❺ ○   ❻ ○
❼ ✕   ❽ ○   ❾ ✕

🐸 말하기 문제 ············· 39p

❶ tree ❷ sleep ❸ shout
❹ mouse ❺ zebra ❻ lion

🐱 읽기 문제 ··············· 40p

❶ mouse ❷ say ❸ net
❹ king ❺ sleepy ❻ laugh
❼ animal ❽ run ❾ little

🐸 쓰기 문제 ··············· 41p

❶ t r ee ❷ e y e
❸ ki n g ❹ e at
❺ ne t ❻ z ebra
❼ l a ugh ❽ he a r
❾ sa y ❿ lio n

⑪ s l ee p ⑫ m ous e
⑬ n o se ⑭ sh ou t
⑮ o pen ⑯ an i ma l
⑰ littl e ⑱ s lee p y
⑲ c ut ⑳ r u n

표현 익히기

🐸 듣기 문제 ················· 44p

(듣기대본)

❶(a) I'm really sorry.
 (b) Oh, thank you.

❷(a) I'm too sleepy.
 (b) I'm really sorry.

❸(a) Let me go, please.
 (b) You are a little mouse.

❹(a) It's my mistake.
 (b) Don't worry.

❺(a) You are a little mouse.
 (b) I'm the king of all the animals.

정답

❶ (a)   ❷ (a)   ❸ (a)   ❹ (b)   ❺ (a)

말하기 문제 ⋯⋯⋯⋯⋯⋯⋯ 45p

❶ Oh, thank you.
❷ Let me go, please.
❸ I'm too sleepy.
❹ I'm the king of all the animals.

읽기 문제 ⋯⋯⋯⋯⋯⋯⋯ 46p

❶ Oh, thank you.
❷ Let me go, please.
❸ You are a little animal.
❹ I'm really sorry.
❺ I'm too sleepy.

쓰기 문제 ⋯⋯⋯⋯⋯⋯⋯ 47p

❶ It's my mistake.
❷ Let me go, please.
❸ Don't worry.
❹ I'm the king of all the animals.
❺ I'm really sorry.

Dictation

50p-51p

❶ tree ❷ nose ❸ eye ❹ mouse
❺ shout ❻ I'm really sorry
❼ Let me go, please.

52p-53p

❶ laugh ❷ little ❸ king
❹ eat ❺ I'm too sleepy now.

54p-55p

❶ Oh, thank you ❷ run
❸ zebra ❹ net

56p-57p

❶ shout ❷ shout ❸ hear ❹ run

58p-59p

❶ Don't worry. ❷ cut
❸ mouse ❹ lion ❺ little

스토리 이해하기 ⋯⋯⋯⋯⋯ 60p-63p

A ❶ ① × ② ○ ③ ×
　 ❷ ① ○ ② × ③ ×

B ❶ ② ❷ ③

C ❶ ① king ② eat ③ say ④ sleepy
　 ❷ ① zebra ② net

D ❶ The zebra is sleeping.
　 ❷ The mouse yawns.
　 ❸ The cat is following the mouse.
　 ❹ The dog tries to escape.

175

The Sun and the Wind

〈68p-69p〉

The sun and the wind are arguing with each other.
"I'm stronger than you," says the sun.
"I'm much stronger than you,"
says the wind.

해와 바람은 서로 다투고 있어요.

"나는 너보다 더 강해." 해가 말해요.
"내가 너보다 훨씬 강해."
바람이 말해요.

〈70p-71p〉

"I can break down a house," says the wind.
"And I can blow a ship across the sea.
What can you do?" asks the wind.

"나는 집을 무너뜨릴 수 있어." 바람이 말해요.
"그리고 나는 배를 바다 너머로 불어버릴 수도 있어.
너는 무엇을 할 수 있니?" 바람이 물어요.

〈72p-73p〉

"That isn't my style," says the sun.
"I can make the flowers bloom.
And I help the trees to grow."
"Pah! That's child's play," says the wind.
"In a test of strength, I'd beat you."

"그것은 내 스타일이 아니야." 라고 해가 말해요.
"나는 꽃들을 피울 수 있어.
그리고 나무가 자라는 것을 돕지."
"흥! 그것은 어린이 장난이지." 라고 바람이 말해요.
"힘겨루기 시합을 하면, 내가 너를 이길 거야."

〈74p-75p〉

The wind sees a man walking along the road.
The wind says, "Let's have a match.
Whoever takes off that man's coat wins."
"All right," says the sun.

바람은 길을 따라 걷고 있는 남자를 봐요.

바람은 말해요, "우리 시합을 하자."
저 남자의 외투를 벗기는 자가 이기는 거야."
"좋아." 해가 동의해요.

〈76p-77p〉

"I'll start first," says the wind.
"He will take off his coat soon."
And the wind blows a powerful wind.
But the man grabs his coat tightly.

"내가 먼저 할게." 바람이 말해요.
"그는 곧 그의 외투를 벗을 거야."
그리고 바람은 강력한 바람을 불어요.
그러나 남자는 그의 외투를 꽉 잡아요.

〈78p-79p〉

The wind takes a deep breath.
And the wind blows with all his energy.
But the man grabs his coat tighter.
At last, the wind gives up.

바람은 깊은 숨을 쉬어요.
그리고 모든 힘을 모아 바람을 불어요.
그러나 남자는 외투를 더 꽉 잡아요.
드디어, 바람은 포기해요.

〈80p-81p〉

"My turn," says the sun.
And the sun begins to shine.
The man feels hotter and hotter.

"내 차례야." 해는 말해요.
그리고 해는 빛을 비추기 시작해요.
남자는 점점 더 덥게 느껴져요.

〈82p-83p〉

His face is as red as a tomato.
He can't stand any more heat.
So he takes off his coat.

그의 얼굴은 토마토처럼 빨개져요.
그는 더 이상 열기를 참지 못해요.
그래서 그는 외투를 벗어요.

〈84p-85p〉

He also takes off his hat.
He arrives at a lake.
He takes off his socks and shoes.
And he dives into the water.

그는 그의 모자도 벗어요.
그는 호수에 도착해요.
그는 양말과 신발도 벗어요.
그리고 그는 물속으로 뛰어 들어가요.

〈86p-87p〉

"Well?" says the sun with a smiling face.
"All right, all right," says the wind.
"You win."
The wind disappears.

"어때?" 해가 웃는 얼굴로 말해요.
"그래, 그래." 바람이 말해요.
"네가 이겼어."
바람은 사라져버려요.

낱말 익히기

🎧 듣기 문제 ·················· 92p

(듣기대본)

❶ wind ❷ hat ❸ tomato

❹ walk ❺ socks ❻ face

정답 ·

❶ 두번째 그림 ❷ 두번째 그림 ❸ 첫번째 그림

❹ 첫번째 그림 ❺ 첫번째 그림 ❻ 두번째 그림

🐷 말하기 문제 ·················93p

❶ sun ❷ ship ❸ house

❹ sea ❺ child ❻ man

❼ road

📖 읽기 문제 ·················· 94p

❶ child ❷ coat ❸ tomato

❹ hat ❺ test ❻ sun

❼ water ❽ grow ❾ flower

✏️ 쓰기 문제 ·················· 95p

❶ house ❷ test ❸ sun

❹ red ❺ hat ❻ road

❼ shoes ❽ water ❾ man

❿ wind ⓫ tomato ⓬ coat

⓭ walk ⓮ child ⓯ socks

⓰ sea ⓱ flower ⓲ face

⓳ ship ⓴ grow

표현 익히기

🎧 듣기 문제 ·················· 98p

(듣기대본)

❶ He takes off his coat.

❷ Let's have a match.

❸ My turn.

❹ I help the trees to grow.

❺ I'm stronger than you.

정답 ·

3

5, 2

1, 4

🐷 말하기 문제 ·················99p

❶ I'm stronger than you.

❷ I help the trees to grow.

❸ Let's have a match.

❹ My turn.

📖 읽기 문제 ··················100p

❶ coat ❷ match

❸ stronger ❹ trees

✏️ 쓰기 문제 ·················· 101p

❶ What can you do?

❷ I can break down a house.

❸ I'm stronger than you.

④ I'd beat you.
⑤ He takes off his coat.

Dictation

104p-105p

❶ sun ❷ I'm stronger than you

❸ wind ❹ house ❺ sea

❻ What can you do?

106p-107p

❶ flower ❷ grow ❸ I'd beat you

❹ man ❺ road

❻ Let's have a match. ❼ sun

108p-109p

❶ coat ❷ wind

❸ man ❹ wind

110p-111p

❶ My turn ❷ sun ❸ man

❹ face ❺ tomato

❻ he takes off his coat

112p-113p

❶ hat ❷ socks ❸ shoes ❹ water

❺ face ❻ wind

스토리 향하기 ········ **114p-117p**

A ❶ ① × ② ○ ③ ×
　 ❷ ① ○ ② × ③ ○

B ❶ ② ❷ ②

C ❶ ① can ② ship ③ wind
　 ❷ ① flower ② grow ③ child

D ❶ The child takes off his socks.
　 ❷ A man arrives at the sea.
　 ❸ She will take off her hat.
　 ❹ I'm taller than you.

The Country Mouse and the City Mouse

〈122p-123p〉

The country mouse and the city mouse are cousins.
One day, the country mouse invites his cousin.
He writes a letter, "Come to my house."

시골 쥐와 도시 쥐는 사촌이에요.

어느 날, 시골 쥐가 그의 사촌을 초대해요.

그는 편지를 써요. "우리 집으로 와."

〈124p-125p〉

The city mouse wears nice clothes.
And he visits the country mouse.
The country mouse greets him.
"Welcome to my home."

도시 쥐는 좋은 옷을 입어요.
그리고 그는 시골 쥐를 방문해요.
시골 쥐는 그를 반갑게 맞아요.
"우리 집에 온 걸 환영해."

〈126p-127p〉

The country mouse puts out some beans and fruit.
"You must be hungry. Help yourself."
The city mouse eats the food.
But he thinks, "I don't like this plain food."

시골 쥐는 콩들과 과일을 내와요.

"너는 분명히 배가 고플거야. 마음껏 먹어."
도시 쥐는 음식을 먹어요.
하지만 그는 생각해요. "이런 평범한 음식은 싫어."

〈128p-129p〉

After lunch, they take a walk in the woods.
The city mouse thinks,
"It's too dull in the country."
He says, "Let's go to the city."

점심 식사 후에, 그들은 숲 속을 산책해요.
도시 쥐는 생각해요.
"시골에 있는 것은 너무 지루해."
그는 말해요. "도시로 가자."

〈130p-131p〉

The country mouse goes to the city.
He sees lots of cars.
The country mouse thinks,
"It's too dangerous here."

시골 쥐는 도시로 가요.
그는 차가 많이 있는 것을 봐요.
시골 쥐는 생각해요.
"여기는 너무 위험해."

180

〈132p-133p〉

They walk though the streets.
Suddenly, a dog runs after them.
They run away from the dog.

그들은 거리를 걸어요.
갑자기, 개가 그들을 쫓아와요.
그들은 개한테서 도망쳐요.

〈134p-135p〉

At last, they arrive at his house.
He lives in a big house.
"What a big house!"
says the country mouse.

드디어, 그들은 그의 집에 도착해요.
그는 커다란 집에 살아요.
"정말 큰 집이구나!"
시골 쥐는 말해요.

〈136p-137p〉

They go to the kitchen.
There is a cake, meat, and cheese.
The city mouse says, "Help yourself."
"Thank you. It looks delicious."
The country mouse begins to eat.

그들은 부엌으로 가요.
케이크와 고기, 그리고 치즈가 있어요.
도시 쥐가 말해요. "마음껏 먹어."
"고마워. 맛있어 보여."
시골 쥐는 먹기 시작해요.

〈138p-139p〉

Just then, someone opens the door.
And people come to the table.
The city mouse shouts, "Follow me!"
They run away to a small hole.

바로 그때, 누군가가 문을 열어요.
그리고 사람들이 식탁으로 와요.
도시 쥐는 소리쳐요. "나를 따라 와!"
그들은 작은 구멍으로 도망가요.

〈140p-141p〉

The country mouse says,
"I'll go back to the country.
Though I eat only beans,
I want to have a peaceful life."

시골 쥐는 말해요.
"나는 시골로 돌아갈 거야.
나는 콩 밖에 먹지 못하더라도,
평화스럽게 살고 싶어.

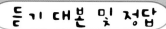 듣기 대본 및 정답

낱말 익히기

🐶 듣기 문제 ·················· 146p

(듣기대본)

❶ (a) country　(b)city
❷ (a) cheese　(b) meat
❸ (a) tree　(b) woods
❹ (a) door　(b) nose
❺ (a) letter　(b) man
❻ (a) car　(b) ship
❼ (a) eat　(b) write
❽ (a) bean　(b) fruit
❾ (a) house　(b) kitchen

정답 ··················

❶ b　❷ b　❸ b
❹ a　❺ a　❻ a
❹ b　❺ a　❻ b

🐨 말하기 문제 ·················· 147p

❶ big　❷ small　❸ dog
❹ hungry　❺ cheese　❻ fruit
❼ cake

📖 읽기 문제 ·················· 148p

❶ cousin　❷ dog　❸ city
❹ letter　❺ table　❻ hungry
❼ food　❽ door　❾ small

🐷 쓰기 문제 ·················· 149p

❶ country　❷ cousin　❸ letter
❹ bean　❺ fruit　❻ hungry
❼ food　❽ car　❾ door
❿ table　⓫ small　⓬ dog
⓭ city　⓮ kitchen　⓯ cheese
⓰ write　⓱ big　⓲ cake
⓳ meat　⓴ woods

표현 익히기

🐶 듣기 문제 ·················· 152p

(듣기대본)

❶ (a) Help yourself.
　(b) I don't like this plain food.
❷ (a) Welcome to my home.
　(b) What a big house!
❸ (a) I'll go back to the country.
　(b) Let's go to the city.

정답 ··················

❶ b, a　❷ a, b　❸ b, a

❶ Help yourself.
   It looks delicious!
❷ Welcome to my home.
   What a big house!

❶ ② ❷ ① ❸ ① ❹ ①

❶ Let's go to the city.
❷ What a big house!
❸ It looks delicious.
❹ It's too dangerous here.
❺ Welcome to my house.

Dictation

158p-159p

❶ country ❷ mouse
❸ city ❹ country
❺ Welcome to my home.

160p-161p

❶ fruit ❷ Help yourself. ❸ food
❹ woods ❺ mouse
❻ Let's go to the city.

162p-163p

❶ city ❷ car ❸ country
❹ It's too dangerous here.
❺ walk ❻ dog

164p-165p

❶ big ❷ What a big house!
❸ mouse ❹ kitchen ❺ cake
❻ cheese ❼ It looks delicious.

166p-167p

❶ door ❷ table ❸ small
❹ country ❺ bean

A ❶ ① ○ ② ○ ③ ×
   ❷ ① × ② ○ ③ ×

B ❶ ③ ❷ ②

C ❶ ① city ② car ③ country
   ❷ ① walk ② dog ③ run

D ❶ The child opens the door.
   ❷ He writes a letter.
   ❹ They take a walk in the woods.
   ❺ They run away from the dog.

이솝우화

부록카드

lion

사자

sleep

tree

nose

open

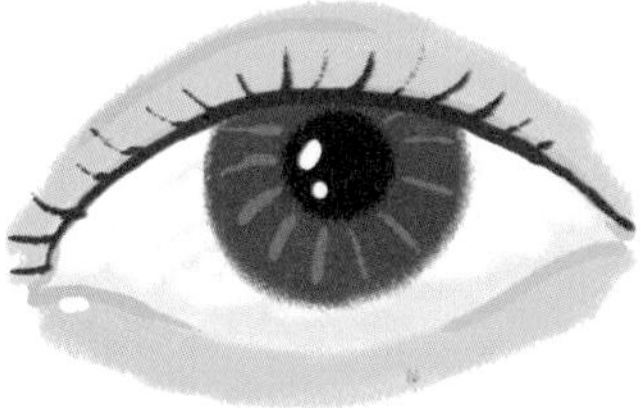

eye

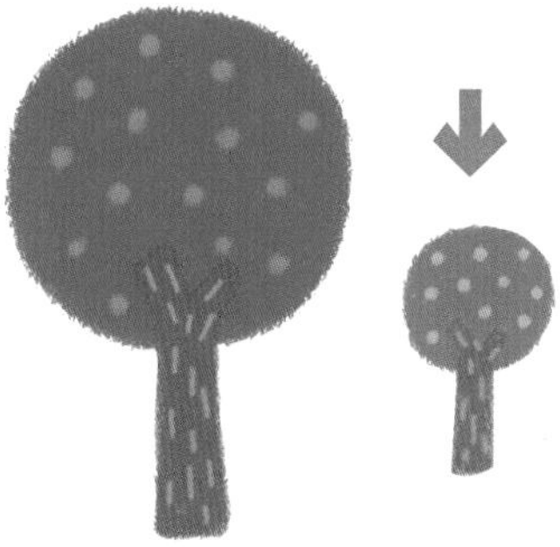

little

mouse

shout

say

잠을 자다

sleep

사자

lion

코

nose

나무

tree

눈

eye

(눈을) 뜨다

open

쥐

mouse

작은

little

말하다

say

소리치다

shout

laugh

animal

king

eat

sleepy

run

zebra

net

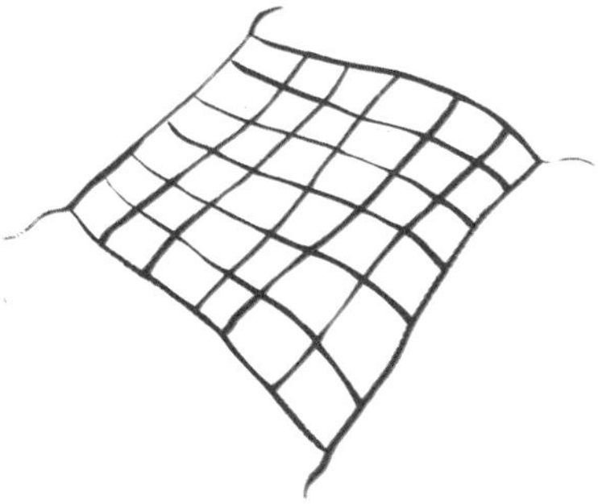

hear

cut

동물
animal

웃다
laugh

먹다
eat

왕
king

달리다
run

졸린
sleepy

그물
net

얼룩말
zebra

자르다
cut

듣다
hear

 sun

 wind

 house

 ship

 sea

 flower

 grow

 child

 test

 man

바람
wind

해
sun

배
ship

집
house

꽃
flower

바다
sea

어린이
child

자라다
grow

남자
man

시험
test

walk

road

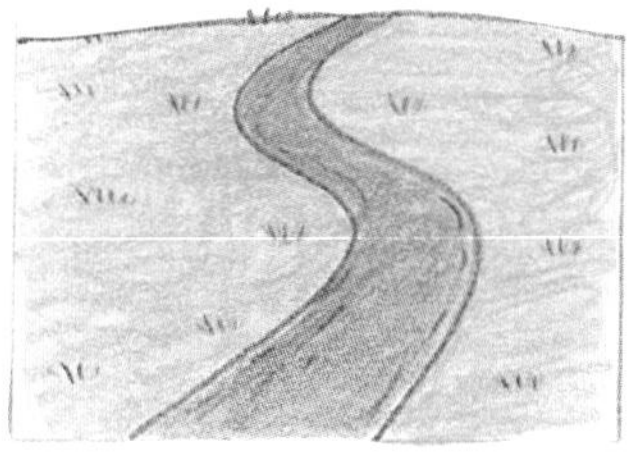

coat

face

red

tomato

hat

socks

shoes

water

길

road

걷다

walk

얼굴

face

외투

coat

토마토

tomato

빨간색

red

양말

socks

모자

hat

물

water

구두

shoes

country

city

cousin

write

letter

bean

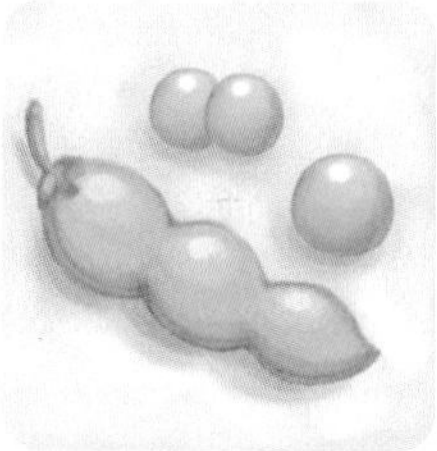

fruit

hungry

food

woods

도시

city

시골

country

쓰다

write

사촌

cousin

콩

bean

편지

letter

배고픈

hungry

과일

fruit

숲

woods

음식

food

car

dog

big

kitchen

cake

meat

cheese

door

table

small

개

dog

자동차

car

부엌

kitchen

커다란

big

고기

meat

케이크

cake

문

door

치즈

cheese

작은

small

탁자

table

I'm really sorry.

It's my mistake.

Let me go, please.

You are a little animal.

I'm the king of all the animals.

I'm too sleepy.

Oh, thank you.

Don't worry.

I'm stronger than you.

I can break down a house.

What can you do?

I help the trees to grow.

제 잘못이에요.

정말 죄송해요.

너는 작은 동물이야.

저를 가게 해주세요.

나는 지금 너무 졸린다.

나는 모든 동물의 왕이다.

걱정하지 마세요.

오, 고마워요.

나는 집을 무너뜨릴 수 있어.

나는 너보다 강해.

나는 나무를 자라게 도와.

너는 무엇을 할 수 있니?

I'd beat you.

Let's have a match.

My turn.

He takes off his coat.

Welcome to my home.

Help yourself.

I don't like this plain food.

Let's go to the city.

It's too dangerous here.

What a big house!

It looks delicious.

I'll go back to the country.

우리 시합을 하자.

나는 너를 이길 거야.

그는 외투를 벗어요.

내 차례야.

많이 먹어.

우리 집에 온 걸 환영해.

우리 도시로 가자.

나는 이런 평범한 음식은 싫어.

정말 큰 집이다!

여기는 너무 위험해.

나는 시골로 돌아갈 거야.

맛있어 보인다.